The TOOTH Book

By

Theo. LeSieg

Illustrated by

Roy McKie

COLLINS

BRIGHT and EARLY Books for BEGINNING Beginners

Trademark of Random House, Inc., William Collins Sons & Co. Ltd., Authorised User

Conditions of Sale

The paperback edition of this book is sold subject to the condition that it shall not, by way of trade or otherwise, be lent, re-sold, hired out or otherwise circulated without the publisher's prior consent in any form of binding or cover other than that which it is published and without a similar condition including this condition being imposed on the subsequent purchaser.

ISBN 0 00 171227 6 (hardback)
ISBN 0 00 171285 3 (paperback)

Text copyright © 1981 by Dr. Seuss and A. S. Geisel
Illustrations Copyright © 1981 by Random House Inc.
A Bright and Early Book for Beginning Beginners
Published by arrangement with Random House Inc. New York, New York
First published in Great Britain 1982
Printed & bound in Hong Kong

2 3 4 5 6 7 8 9 10

Who has teeth?

Well . . .
look around
and you'll find out who.
You'll find
that red-headed uncles do.

Policemen do.
And zebras too.

And unicycle riders do.

And camels
and their drivers do!

Even little girls named Ruthie
all have teeth.
All Ruths are toothy.

Teeth!
You find them everywhere!
On mountaintops!
And in the air!

And if you care
to poke around,
you'll even find them
underground.

You'll find them
east, west, north, and south.
You'll find them
in a lion's mouth.

TEETH!
They are very much in style.

They must be
very much
worthwhile!

"They come in handy
when you chew,"
says Mr. Donald Driscoll Drew.

"They come in handy
when you smile,"
says Smiling Sam
the crocodile.

"They come in handy
in my job,"
says high trapezer
Mike McCobb.

"If I should ever
lose a tooth,
I'd lose my wife.
And that's the truth."

"Teeth come in handy
when you speak,"
says news broadcaster
Quincy Queek.

"Without my teeth
I'd talk like ducks,
and only broadcast
quacks and klucks."

"You're lucky
that you have your teeth,"
says a sad, sad snail
named Simon Sneeth.

"I don't have one!
I can never smile
like Smiling Sam the crocodile."

"Clams have no teeth,"
says Pam the clam.
"I cannot eat
hot dogs
or ham."

"No teeth at all,"
says Pam the clam.
"I cannot eat
roast leg of lamb.
Or peanuts! Pizzas!
Popcorn! Spam!
Not even huckleberry jam!"

"Without teeth
we can't play trombones,"
says a jellyfish named Jimbo Jones.

"I have no teeth,"
says Hilda Hen.
"But women do.
And so do men.

"So I have happy
news for you.
You will grow two sets!
Set one. Set two."

"You will lose
set number one.
And when you do,
it's not much fun.

"But then you'll grow
set number two!
32 teeth, and all brand new.
16 downstairs, and 16 more
upstairs on the upper floor.

"And when you get your second set,
THAT'S ALL THE TEETH·
YOU'LL EVER GET!"

SO . . .
don't chew down trees
like beavers do.
If you try,
you'll lose set
number two!

And . . .
don't be dumb
like Mr. Glotz.
Don't break your teeth
untying knots!

And don't be dumb
like Katy Klopps.
Don't try to chew off
bottle tops!

Don't gobble junk
like Billy Billings.
They say his teeth
have fifty fillings!

They sure are handy
when you smile.
So keep your teeth
around awhile.

And <u>never</u> bite your dentist
when he works inside your head.

Your dentist is
your teeth's best friend.

Bite someone else instead!